A Floe of Life

also by E S Cuny

These Are Good Poems

Halloween, Fireside,. or Just Plain Weird Poems

A Floe of Life

by

E.S. Cuny

A Floe of Life
Copyright © 2022
by Eugene S. Cuny

Published by Kallisto Gaia Press Inc.
First Edition

Kallisto Gaia Press Inc.
801 E. 51st St.
Austin TX 78723
Phone: 512.654.7205
www.kallistogaiapress.org

Cover: *Typewriter and Mirror* by author.
Author's portrait by Herbert Long
ISBN: 978-1-952224-22-5

For you who came before,
and all who are around now
to those who are coming after –
you made this work.
– Thanks!

A Floe of Life

by

E.S. Cuny

Table of Contents

Owls

I have my grandmother's porcelain owls

they're nestled together under the shelves,

holding coffee, flour and things sweet and sour

while keeping the kitchen under protective spells.

Nothing fancy you know, there's little to show

they just sit silently to see that all is well.

Sifting through one laden with herbs and teas,

sniffing an aroma quite nice of a particular spice

brings suddenly back a fond memory:

How she would pass on lore while making decisions galore,

keeping a conversational tone while baking up scones,

taking up a position that made the counter her throne.

Interesting how traditions from across the sea

when kept, can make the kitchen into the heart of a family.

ODE TO RASPBERRY JAM

It's not like Strawberry – which is everybody's favorite –
with its plump berry fullness fulfilling taste buds',
Desires.

And it's not like Blueberry – which is also everybody's favorite –
with its slick skein of luscious darkness sliding towards,
Delight.

Nor is it like the Calico Peach – the families' special secret. No,
Raspberry is relegated to the back of the uppermost shelf,
forgotten,

only taken down when the others are gone and there's nothing else left.
Then, coming out of the cold down from the upper corner, the winter
Wind

races through the Northern forests, across frozen farmers fields
tinging the very roots of the plant with traces of blizzards' grit,
Embedding

in the bittersweet berry. There to be slathered with butter
over steaming hot scones on a Minnesota morning
in a grandma's kitchen
far, far away.

MY MOM

My mom was really great
even way past eighty eight
(which is when a lot of old timers start
to have a major change of heart.)
But she would never look for a flaw
in any of her sons' daughters-in-law.
Although I, sure, was a different situation
one which gave her much aggravation.
                Oh well.

Dry Winter's Day

On a dry winter's day, sound carries
over barren fields flecked with snow,
rings out around a barn, resounding inside,
sonorous among the intended implements
upended and waiting. Outside a hammer bangs
      ringing anvil and steel.

An old hinge is straightened, thrown on a pile.
He turns to extending old lumber a bit farther.
Cold air scrapes in short thick puffs,
hammer rising hammer falling,
pounding out nails, sweating hands leaving
      vaporous trails.

His scratchy voice sings with the cacophony,
"Can't you see my hands are burning?"
he sings out loud, as if she could hear. But
she wasn't there. Pneumatic doors had shut
and here he was. His sight blurred,
      hammer hit wood.

"Can't you see, my eyes are burning?"
he whisper-sang to no one in particular.
With a sigh he turns to pulling rusty nails;
old boards resonate in dissonance,
amplifying creaky withdrawal.
      He had left it all,

now argued with his father, who wanted his sons
working the mines as had he, and his fathers before.
He thought of his time in the mines,
of the lantern's glint on fresh scrapped coal;
there, a footprint in Carboniferous era, here,
            a silvery patterned fern.

A million years in flakes lay glistening
on the cavern's floor. He thought of the miners
lined up in owner's harnesses, going down
to cut black diamonds from the black forest.
He had been in the diamond, and the way out
                  shone.

He pauses, looks around at the white liming covering all,
gives a pull, and nail gives to the hammer's claw.
"Can't you see my soul is burning!" and laughs out loud.
Then he turns boards together, and again the hammer flies.
The air, crisp and clear, reverberates in vibrations as steel
is driven into wood, and repurposed lumber is again
                  made good.

DAWNING GRAVITAS

I. Coupling to Sleep

After all that … then,
        a mingling of toes,
an adjustment of pillows,
        a matching of breaths,
a cupping of breasts,
        a smiling quirk,
an elbow jerk
        in subconscious traces
while slinking away
        into oblivion's embraces.

II. At Touch of Dawn

Moving now at the touch of dawn
still half in half out of last night,
coming awake over coffee and toast,
thinking how love moves as it will,
perhaps giving to us what wills
we may inhabit. On this morning
I miss your presence I miss, simply,
your company at this table.
And I have to leave this fading grace
and turn daylight into something useful.

‘

III. Q and A

All kinds of answers float around
from "Possiblys" to "Laters" or "Not right nows",
to the "It can wait" or "I just can't see"
and the always awkward, "Why do it anyhow?"

And "Perhapses" come by the hundreds,
and the "Maybes" will drive you insane,
the "Why what fors?" are scorchers,
and the "Nos" will fall like rain.

But Yeses come few and far between
emerging as from an envelope,
in an anticipation permeating the atmosphere
and gives away much more than is ever spoke.

But now's the time to say out loud for all the world to hear
that word which is to my soul, oh so dreadfully dear.

VI. The Wedding Toast

Here's to the couple
who are making viable
a past, present and future
by embracing tradition,
encompassing community,
and engaging with that mystery
we know as life …

Just don't get too lost
in all that gravitas.
    – Amen!

Angel Grace

       Angel Grace
won't you ground zero right here in on me?
I'm ready, with my feet on the ground,
I'm taking a hard look around,
overwhelmed by all that I see.

       Angel Freight,
you can drop that semi's load down on me,
this is the life I own willingly
where together we will raise a family
and make a home in serenity.

       Angel Bright,
you've given me a feeling to my boots
and given us a future and history,
linked with the long line of family,
we have a place for new life to root,

where we will sustain a hope and faith
in a redeeming human race, thank you,
       Angel Grace.

BIRTHING CENTERS

Stopping by the Neonatal Care room on the way out
after a long and protracted but successful birth,
one cannot help but marvel at the bustle and sound,
of nurses tending to babes as over cradles they perch.
Some move cubicle to cubicle, while others bring new ones in
to be bathed and swathed, and then out to rejoin their mothers.
Some are brought to the partition glass for families to see. Proudly we
wave, coo and point out ours to any and all others,
exchanging congratulations and salutations all around.
Already the fraught filled hours are fading away,
already the future is calling us back. One last glance —
at the constant activity among creches in symmetrical array
amid the sibilant susurration of muted infants' cries —
I come away smiling with the image of a buzzing beehive!

Necklines

I'm staring at the line of my son's neck
as he naps in the front passenger seat,
while returning from a visit to Corpus Christi,
a farewell to grandma before off he goes into the
                    Service.

That line of his neck is the only exposed portion
of his body from my point of view, a line running
from collar to cap, not the most remarkable
nor the most familiar-izable stretch,
            but …

I realize it is a young man's neck,
long, and strong, vertebrae visible
underneath a light covering of fuzz.
The neck straightens out, lengthens
            and marches

on up into the top, merging under tangled curls.
A neck I have many times wanted to ring
or insisted be washed – yes, again! – or be dressed
or buttoned down or adorned with a tie.
            A neck,

I'd like to be able to hold and hug right now.
There's a long line of tradition in that stretch
a familial line that goes way back, to whenever.
A line that I too must uphold, a line I cannot cross.
          So I drive,

content, proud, fearful; struck by that fragile point
of all that strength, stretched out in a thin line
that connects musculature to decisive thought.
That neck which is leaving our home,
          on its own,

for good or better or worse. I sense,
my own connection slipping,
oh! how I'm going to miss him.
My hand rises, falls back, let him sleep.
          He's going to need it.

HATS OFF

I lost my hat.
It was only a hat.
But my favorite one.
Funny how we get so attached
to impersonal personal things. I was invited
by my son and his friend to go floating
with them down the river. Off we went,
into the water, funneled through rapids,
over rocky swells, thinking great day,
great river, hot sun glad I had my hat
as we tumbled into the water and schloop!
the current tugged it off and pulled it away,
for an instant floating just out of reach.
I could stretch out and grab it back
or let it go, catch it over the edge
in the riffling flow, a fun challenge
in a fun day. I accepted.
        I lost my hat.

It wasn't there.
I scoured back water eddies,
whirlpools, reeds and rocky shallows. Nada.
All I had had to do was reach over and grab it.
Then I would have had it close, not let it go off,
and even kept the shape I'd molded it in.
We all look but can't find it,
so we keep on floating
down and away
        and continue the fun.

At their camp, I leave them
after a couple of beers, and vodka shots
and stogies out the wazoo.
I could have grabbed another one and stayed.
But they don't need the old man hanging around.
A bit of privacy in their own world is a good thing,
not having to guard their stories, jokes and dreams.
It's a challenge to let them go on their own
a risk you've got to master and try,
       to catch them on the other side.

Ode to a Voyager

11-11-80
nearing Saturn closest approach
one million plus K
Titan 700,000 K
approaching @ 59,000 K/h

11-13-80
210 K away and leaving
124 K above clouds closest approach.

Rings like rainbows.
Spokes like sheen.

This in our
Year of the Colt.

Now going 30°N of ecliptic
by 1990 should be past Pluto
and entering deep space.

To one of the highest
aspirations
of mankind,
       Farewell.

At Christmas Dinner

This is a Prayer of Thanks
to whichever great spirit of compassion
each of us turns to in times of need,
or in desperation or in darkness,
when we seek solace
from that sense of being, so,
to that sense of a gathering
 greater than ourselves, we are thankful.
We are thankful for this repast
before us and the light in this moment.
We ask for a blessing on all gathered here
as we in turn give light to the memories
of those not with us today,
as we remember the many things
done for us this past year
and look forward to the coming one.
May we carry forth with love, forgiveness
and hope in our hearts.
In recognition of this we say to all:
'Thank you everyone, you're welcome.'
– Amen.

Way Stations of the Heart

Well, my grandson came for his summer vacation,
dropped off by his folks as many will do,
hoping for relief from the trials and tribulations
of one thoroughly into the "Terrible Twos".

Boy, he'd run, run, run around, open every drawer,
push all the buttons on every device he found,
leaving a trail of debris all over the floor
on his path to the bath where he'd flush things down!

He would play his music player REAL REAL LOUD
and march-march-march with all the exuberance of life.
He'd wave finger-tipped raspberries oh-so-proud,
and ask the never ending questions: why, why, why?

Oh he stopped my heart in the park at Shipe:
 he broke for the pool and jumped right in –
with no warning or wings, just a squeal of delight –
and got hauled out wearing a great big grin.

Well, his parents came for their two legged riot.
Now things around here … sure are quiet.

WHIRLING HOPES

From seeing her peeking out under a blanket
that tucked her deep into her stroller,
to watching her dance around a room
when only a year or more older,
and now in a high pitchedy voice
and with precise elocution,
she orders me and the dog around
while spinning in yet, another revolution.

They should name a hurricane after her
for this granddaughter's cascading twirls
leaves glittery debris from a flurry of glee
in the wake of her balletic swirls.

And in all the wishes there are for this little girl
I sense too, the hopes we all have for a better world.

Old-Timer's Siri-Us Blues

I got a smart phone they said it's the best one of all.
My kids told me just text them so they won't have to call.
It's got a lot of buttons which are just geeky to me,
sometimes I push them and get an emoji.
I'm so lost in icons I'm in an electronic Hell,
if I ask Siri she sends a Smiley with an L.O.L.

They say it can do the internet and play music too,
you can play games on it or find the price of a shoe.
You can take pictures, make movies or a Facebook post,
get answers to questions like, "who loves you the most?"
They say it has more memory than sent men to the moon,
so now I can use it to watch my favorite cartoons.

What happened to make my Princess phone wrong?
You could talk on a cord about a half a mile long.
They'll make fun of it by sending me a Frowny Face,
but the best thing about it was it always stayed in one place.
Now I have a question which is wracking my brain:
Why oh why does Siri, want to drive me insane?

On Down a Road

Running down the highway at eighty miles an hour,
the road still slick and wet from a passing thunder shower.
Glimpsed ahead the bowing shape of Granite Mountain's ridge,
looming over the humph-back grid of the Llano River's bridge.

Over it all a rainbow curves, then lightening strikes overhead.
I begin a skid in a winding bend kicking gravel from the edge.
Four arches are calling out in an extended visual rhyme,
four easy steps to heaven: road, bridge, rock and arc, all in a line.

Releasing the wheel I can leave this field and tumble into the sky
 —then a thunder clap with a mighty slap jerks the car from side to side.
I glance in the back at the package sacks, and cut back in with a sigh;
it's been a long road, been a tough night, I'm not finished with this ride.

Muttering at the rain, shaking fog from my brain thinking of that load,
I pause for a minute, get under the limit, and roll on down the road.

Things Return to Place

It can start at the end of a party,
a birthday, a broadcast, a *'bon voyage'*.
Too late, too tired to clean it all up – "To bed!
"Leave it", laughingly, "*por le garbage*".
Next day pick up, sweep up, dishes washed,
     leftovers wrapped up,
     frozen or tossed.
Dumping the cups and the urns filled with ash,
sorting the glass and cans from the trash,
and when the tableware is set in its case,
finally a restful minute, a bit of contentment,
     that things have returned to place.

Or it can happen in the middle of a day,
when there's some time alone with others away.
On the radio you'll hear a familiar tune
     that takes you back,
     to a roll in the sack
with a lover you'd long forgot.
What if, you begin to wonder and presume;
then the music stops – whether wanted or not –
and you're staring a mirror hard in the face.
You've come back from the moon, all too soon
     and sigh, as you return to place.

And it can end at the start of a sunset sky,
out on the porch rocking side by side.
In the starry vastness soaring birds cry;
we take each other's hand, I understand,
there's no reason to ask why:
     Did we do as we should?
     Did we raise the kids good?
No not always but we tried,
as memories well up in our eyes.
By luck or by fate, we found God's grace,
from the witnessing of birth to this calling Earth,
serene now in the knowledge that things,
     return to place.

Moonsong

Oh when that sun has gone and set,
and those stars start to shine
and that ribbon of road
just keeps on rolling
rolling, rolling right on up
into the sky, leading the way
      home to you.

Their red towers, aglow over there.
Casting out, into the night air.
What do they tell us of ourselves?
Well I don't know what's right or wrong
inside or outside of me.
      All I know

is the moonbeam's shining, shining
sweeping across midnight pastures,
gliding over silent waters,
dancing along the silv'ry wires,
oh Moonbeam Moonbeam
Moonbeam – won't you dance
      with me?

Dear reader,

I hope you've enjoyed this little chapbook, which continues a theme from earlier works I loosely call 'Personal -Universal' poems. Those previous publications are: *"These Are Good Poems"* and *"Halloween, Fireside, or Just Plain Weird Poems"*, which should be available on your most prolific e-tailer's book section.

This could not have been completed without the very patient participation and excellent editing of Tony Burnett. Through him I am honored to be associated with Kallisto Gaia Press.

Any comments, observations, questions or suggestions are welcome. Please send them to ifandorx9@gmail.com.

Thanks for taking the time.

> - Eugene S.